SABER-TOOTHED

ASHLEY GISH

ICE AGE CREATURES X BOOKS

NORTH AMERICA

EUROPE

ASIA

AFRICA

SOUTH AMERICA

AUSTRALIA

CREATIVE EDUCATION · CREATIVE PAPERBACKS

Published by Creative Education and Creative Paperbacks • P.O. Box 227, Mankato, Minnesota 56002 • Creative Education and Creative Paperbacks are imprints of The Creative Company • www.thecreativecompany.us • Design by Rita Marshall • Production by Dana Kodike • Printed in the United States of America • Photographs by Alamy (Album, All Canada Photos, dbimages, Stocktrek Images, Inc.), Getty Images (DEA PICTURE LIBRARY, Mark Hallett Paleoart), Creative Commons Wikimedia (Prehistoricplanes), iStockphoto (Tommy McNeeley), Deviant Art (true-leveller, Vae1), Prehistoric Fauna (Roman Uchytel), Dreamtime (Jerry Coli), Daniel Eskridge, Shutterstock (Volodymyr Burdiak, Valentyna Chukhlyebova, Kostyantyn Ivanyshen, Milkovasa, Smetana Natasha, Svetsol)

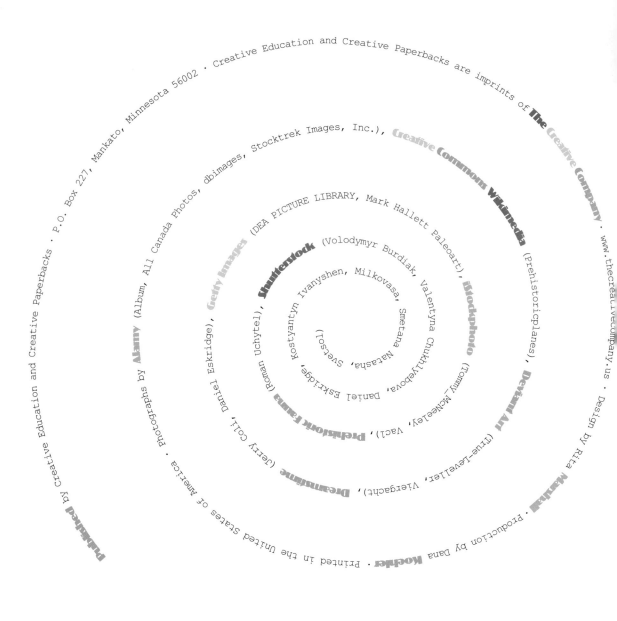

SABER-TOOTHED CATS

CONTENTS

ICE AGE CREATURES
X
BOOKS

XCEPTIONAL ANCIENT ANIMALS

Saber-toothed cats were strong and fierce. Their fangs were like long sabers. They are some of the most popular and well-known Ice Age animals.

Saber-Toothed Cat Basics

Saber-toothed cats were members of the cat family. They are distantly related to lions, cheetahs, tigers, and domestic cats. Saber-toothed cats lived all over the world. Now they are **extinct**. Many of their remains have been found in the eastern United States.

SABER-TOOTHED CAT SPECIES

More than a dozen kinds of saber-toothed cats roamed Earth. They lived all over the world except in the Arctic and Antarctica.

SMILODON

MACHAIRODUS

HOMOTHERIUM

Smilodon (*SMY-luh-don*) was about seven feet (2.1 m) long from head to tail. It stood four feet (1.2 m) tall at the shoulder. It weighed up to 800 pounds (363 kg). This cat had a stubby bobtail. But its canine teeth were long—up to eight inches (20.3 cm)!

   Homotherium (*HO-muh-THEE-ree-um*) was another kind of saber-toothed cat. It is called the scimitar cat. It died out around 28,000 years ago. Its fangs were about four inches (10.2 cm) long. Long legs probably helped this cat run fast.

SHARP SABERS

These curved swords are sharp on one side.

The La Brea Tar Pits in California are made of naturally occurring liquid asphalt. This gooey substance claimed the lives of many Ice Age animals.

Smilodon was twice as heavy as a lion.

HEAVY-WEIGHTS

SABER-TOOTHED CAT BASICS FACT

Many people refer to the saber-toothed cat as a "saber-toothed tiger." But this ancient cat was not a tiger.

TOP FIVE XTREME SABER-TOOTHED CATS

Xtreme Saber-toothed Cat #5

Sticky _Smilodon_ The La Brea Tar Pits hold the remains of many extinct animals. The most common **fossils** found there are from dire wolves. But many are from saber-toothed cats. Thousands of _Smilodon_ fossils have been recovered from the pits. The remains are from animals of all ages. _Smilodon_ would have been attracted to the sticky asphalt. Many plant-eaters became trapped in the pits. When the big cats got too close, they became stuck, too.

Saber-Toothed Cat Beginnings

All true saber-toothed cats belonged to the *Machairodontinae* (*ma-CAIR-uh-DON-tin-EE*) group of felines. This name is Greek for "dagger-toothed." Not all the members of this family had extremely long teeth, though. The most famous saber-toothed cats lived during the last Ice Age. This time period lasted from about 2.6 million to 11,700 years ago. During an ice age, temperatures around the world decreased. Ice covered much of the northern part of Earth. Vast grasslands developed.

Ancient bison and mammoths roamed the grass-lands. Food was plentiful for them. But their presence attracted the attention of large **carnivores**. Saber-toothed cats hunted the large, slow prey.

1842

1881

1888

first *Smilodon* fossil, South America

Smilodon fossil, California

Smilodon skull, Florida

1949 1951

2000

three complete *Homotherium*
skeletons, Texas

Homotherium jawbone,
North Sea

Smilodon had long teeth but weak jaws. Its canine teeth could easily break if the cat bit into hard bones.

Xtreme Saber-toothed
Cat #4

Giants in the Land The oldest saber-toothed cat fossils are from *Megantereon*. They were found in North America and are over 4.5 million years old. A full skeleton of Megantereon was once found in France. These cats were about the size of a modern jaguar. But they weighed as much as 330 pounds (150 kg). Scientists believe they behaved like leopards. After killing large prey, they dragged it into a tree. This kept it away from other animals.

XTRAORDINARY LIFESTYLE

Scientists study extinct animals by looking at their preserved remains.

They compare fossils with the animals' living relatives.

Scientists think saber-toothed cats lived in groups like African lions (pictured) do today.

Saber-Toothed Cat Society

Saber-toothed cats are most similar in lifestyle to
African lions. Like lions, saber-toothed cats may have
cared for sick or injured members of their group.

    Scientists are not sure why saber-toothed cats
grew long canines. These big cats may have used their
long teeth to puncture animals' throats or slice into
their soft bellies. Or these huge teeth could have
been just for show. Competing male cats may have been
intimidated by a rival's dagger-like fangs. Female cats
may have preferred large-toothed males.

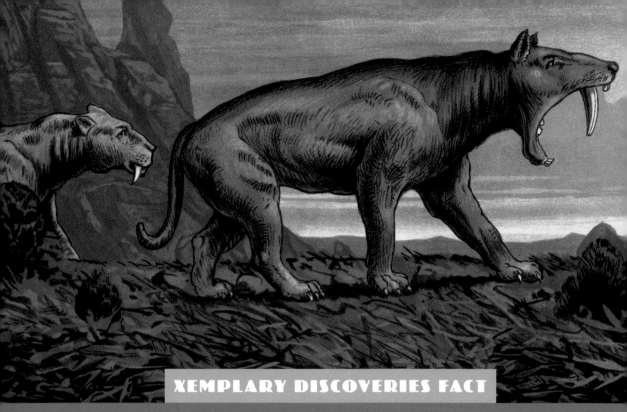

The first mounted *Smilodon* skeleton was displayed in 1910 at the Los Angeles Museum of History, Science, and Art.

XEMPLARY DISCOVERIES

Scientists develop ideas about how saber-toothed cats might have lived. Sometimes, their ideas are wrong. Then they come up with new ones.

All cats are carnivores.

MEAT-EATING FAMILY

People once thought *Smilodon* had extra skin around its mouth. This would have allowed it to open its jaws wide. Scientists tested this idea. They built muscles and skin over the cats' fossilized jaws. This showed that the animal did not need extra skin to achieve a wide bite.

At one time, scientists believed saber-toothed cats died out in Europe around 300,000 years ago. But in 2000, a fishing boat in the North Sea hauled up a strange jawbone. It appeared to be from a big cat. Advanced technology compared the fossil with other animals. Tests revealed the jawbone was from *Homotherium*. It was just 28,000 years old. Experts were shocked. Now they know these cats lived more recently.

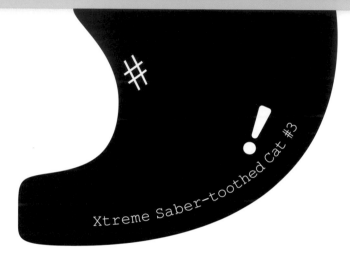

Xtreme Saber-toothed Cat #3

Buried Treasure In 1971, workers were building the First American National Bank in Nashville, Tennessee. After they had dug through 20 feet (6.1 m) of rock, they found a cave. It was filled with dirt. Buried there were teeth and bones from a saber-toothed cat. The findings were preserved. Then they were put on display in the finished building. The state's National Hockey League team took its name—Nashville Predators—from the discovery.

They could grab and hold prey.

BIG PAWS
SHARP CLAWS

XASPERATING CONFLICT

Saber-toothed cats went extinct. But other big cats thrived after the Ice Age.

Saber-Toothed Cat Survival

The large prey animals, such as mammoths and ancient bison, died out. Only small, swift prey remained. Early antelopes and horses were fast. The big cats could not catch them. The smaller, more agile cats that coexisted with the saber-toothed cats were more successful. Saber-toothed cats began dying out. They were gone by the end of the Ice Age.

Early humans were probably afraid of big cats. People are less afraid today. They illegally hunt big cats. Habitat loss and human activity have severely reduced lion and tiger populations. Fewer than 40,000 lions and 4,000 tigers live in the wild. Scientists hope these big cats do not become extinct like saber-toothed cats.

SABER-TOOTHED CAT SURVIVAL FACT

The 28,000-year-old *Homotherium* fossil suggests

early European humans probably encountered the big cats!

Xtreme Saber-toothed Cat #2

Cookie-Cutter Cats *Xenosmilus* (*ZEE-no-SMY-lus*) was first named in the 1980s. Two skeletons were found in Florida. Also at the site were a large number of piglike peccary bones. The cats had short legs and widely spaced teeth. This made researchers think that *Xenosmilus* hunted differently from its relatives. Nicknamed "cookie-cutter cats," they bit chunks of flesh out of the peccaries' flanks. Then they waited for their prey to bleed to death before eating it.

XCITING FACTS

Experts suggest saber-toothed cats were tan or light brown in color. They may have had stripes or spots.

Homotherium roamed in Africa at the same time as our human ancestors. Humans probably avoided contact with such large and fearsome cats.

Most saber-tooth cats hunted by hiding and then leaping on prey, rather than chasing it.

Lions are the only cats that live and hunt in groups. A group of lions is called a pride.

Some saber-toothed cat remains have been found with broken bones. They were likely injured by powerful blows from mammoth tusks.

Tests on *Smilodon* remains from La Brea revealed they are most closely related to African lions and leopards.

A stone sculpture of a *Smilodon* guards the La Plata Museum in La Plata, Argentin A sculpture of two *Smilodons* fighting stands near the La Brea Tar Pits.

Saber-toothed cats competed with dire wolves for food.

All cats, including *Smilodon* and *Homotherium*, share a common ancestor from about 20 million years ago.

Some researchers believe saber-toothed cats took care of weak, injured, or old group members who could no longer hunt.

Tigers and domestic house cats are more closely related to each other than *Smilodon* was to *Homotherium*!

Many modern animals have exaggerated features

they use to impress other animals like themselves.

Xtreme
Saber-toothed Cat #1

Similar Sabertooths The instance of different animals having teeth like sabers is an example of convergent evolution. This means that unrelated animals developed similar features. They may have lived in similar environments but in different parts of the world. A saber-toothed **marsupial** lived about 4 million years ago in South America. A small meat-eating mammal lived more than 40 million years ago in North America. These animals had saber-like teeth but were not related.

GLOSSARY

carnivores – animals that eat meat

extinct – having no living members

fossils – the remains of once-living things preserved in rock

habitat – the natural home of plants and animals

marsupial – an animal whose young is born and grows in a pouch on its mother's body

RESOURCES

"Sabertooth Cat." The Nat: San Diego Natural History Museum. https://www.sdnhm.org/exhibitions/fossil-mysteries/fossil-field-guide-a-z/sabertooth-cat/.

Tite, Jack. *Mega Meltdown: The Weird and Wonderful Animals of the Ice Age*. New York: Blueprint Editions, 2018.

Werdelin, Lars, H. Gregory McDonald, and Christopher A. Shaw, eds. *Smilodon: The Iconic Sabertooth*. Baltimore, Md.: Johns Hopkins University Press, 2018.

INDEX

The first *Smilodon* fossil was found during the 1800s. Scientist Peter Wilhelm Lund gave this saber-toothed cat its name in 1842.